SUDDEN DEATH

ILLUSTRATED HISTORY OF WORLD CUP FOOTBALL AS A MYSTERY THRILLER
Part Four

Arun & Maha

CricketSoccer

This paperback edition first published in 2018
CricketSoccer
www.cricketsoccer.com

Copyright ©Arun and Maha

The right of Arun and Maha to be identified as the authors of this book has been asserted by them in accordance with the Copyright, Design and Patent Acts 1988

ISBN 978-1732522633

All rights reserved. No part of this publication may be reproduced, transmitted, or stored in a retrieval system, in any form or by any means, without permission in writing from CricketSoccer

Acknowledgements

The authors would like to express their sincerest thanks to the whole team associated with CricketSoccer, namely Tim Stannard, Faisal, Vieri Capretta, Paco Polit, Javed Ikbal, Avijit Sen and others, for their continuous support.

They would like to thank Meghana of Shadow Editing Services for her excellent work with the manuscript. Special gratitude to Uli Hesse and Kashinath Bhattacharjee for helping out with their immense knowledge. And finally, many thanks to Tanoy Dutta for his constant faith and encouragement.

Introduction

The history of the World Cup is full of riddles and mysteries. For instance, what happened to the original trophy, the Coupe Jules Rimet? If you scour the internet, you'll read that it was stolen from the headquarters of the Brazilian FA, melted into gold bars and sold. But this is probably nonsense. Pedro Berwanger, the policeman in charge of the investigation, pointed out that the cup as such was a lot more valuable than the gold it was made of. Which is why some people think that the trophy now sits on the shelf of a ruthless collector in some secret location.

Speaking of vanished objects, where is the ball from the 1954 final? The German FA claims it's in their shiny, large museum, but this is highly doubtful. The referee, William Ling, took possession of the ball after the game and for all we know, he still had it when he emigrated to Canada where he died in 1984. Most experts suspect the ball in the museum is from the semi-final or even just a ball used for training.
Men have vanished as well. Where is Joe Gaetjens, the man who scored one of the most famous World Cup goals of all time – the USA's 1-0 against England in 1950? In July 1964, he was arrested by the secret police in his native Haiti. That's the last we heard of him.

There are also numerous less sinister mysteries. What did Materazzi really say to Zidane in 2006? What did really happen to Ronaldo ahead of the 1998 final? Or what about the Mexican wave? We associate it with the 1986 World Cup, hence the name, but there is compelling evidence it was invented in 1981 and by a single man – an American called George Henderson. It should be called the Californian wave, really.
So it was about time that someone sat down to tell the story of the World Cup through riddles and mysteries. Or rather, through a mysterious man who speaks in riddles.

Arun (Arunabha Sengupta) has already proved he is up to the task with a novel in which none other than Sherlock Holmes solves a cricket case. But now, in this book by Arun and Maha, one man's brains are not enough – it takes an entire team of football experts and lovers to solve the riddles mentioned above and help save FIFA's money to ensure the next World Cup can be staged.

It means the book works on many levels. You can read it as a thriller or as a history book – or even as a puzzle book. Can you solve the riddles before FIFA's team can? Could I? Well, that must remain a mystery.

Uli Hesse

The Line up

Herr Fassler : Chief Financial Officer of FIFA, compulsive worrier

Mike Templeton: Football Historian, nibbler nonpareil

Sonja Bjarkardóttir: Genius code breaker, short-lipped and sassy

Javier Hernandez: Interpol Agent, cucumber-calm man of the world

FIFA is in turmoil. On the eve of the 2018 World Cup, the tournament is on the verge of falling through as a crazy football fan holds the organisation at ransom. It is up to these four curious characters to save the day.

With a few days to go for World Cup 2018, FIFA CFO Herr Fassler received a text message that kicked off a curious chain of events.

The systems of the organisation have been hacked into and the entire funds for the World Cup have been transferred to untraceable accounts.

Behind this diabolical manipulation is a football-tragic.

His demands:

A game of 20 questions

- The game will be played in 5 rounds
- Each round will have 4 questions based on the past World Cups
- At the end of each round, if you get all 4 questions correct, 20% of your funds will be transferred back to your account. You will be able to proceed to the next round.
- Any wrong answer **ends** the game. However, the funds already transferred, will remain with FIFA. The rest of the money will be lost.
- Questions will be asked every 2 hours
- Time permitted to answer each question is 15 minutes
- Timer will start automatically on your laptop

- The only way to recover your money and ensure the World Cup goes on exactly as planned is to answer all my questions correctly.

A crack team has been assembled
And they have recovered 60% of their funds by solving 12 questions

You can read all about that in

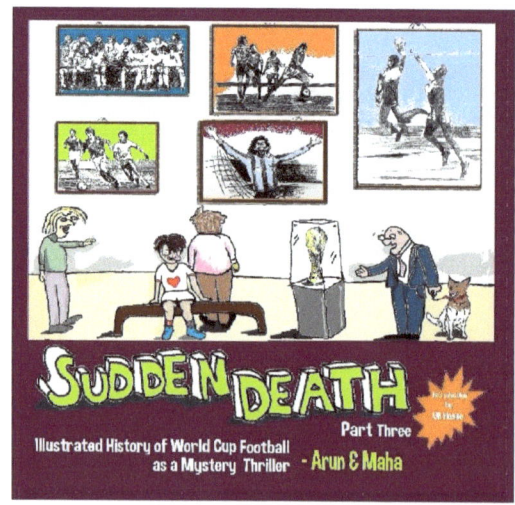

... and now

Ticket prices, Celsius, Altitude alike/There's always TV, spectators can take a hike.

_ _ _ _ _ _ _

Ticket prices, Celsius, Altitude alike/There's always TV, spectators can take a hike.

— — — — — —

1986, Mexico

Merely 16 years after a near disastrous experiment, the Cup was back in Mexico. Of course, Colombia and Brazil pulling out helped their case, but some murky television deals did play the role in the choice.

Yet again there were 24 teams, which meant a second round, effectively the pre-quarter-finals, and long drawn-out schedule.

No one has ever dominated a World Cup as much as the phenomenal Diego Maradona did that year. Perhaps only the Garrincha of 1962 comes close. The Hand of God is infamous, but the feet, especially the left, were even closer to the Divine.

First Round

Group 1

Team	Italy	Bulgaria	South Korea	GF	GA	Pt
Argentina	1-1(1-1)	2-0(0-0)	3-1(2-0)	6	2	5
Italy		1-1 (1-0)	3-2(1-0)	5	4	5
Bulgaria *			1-1(1-0)	2	4	2
South Korea				4	7	1

Group 2

Team	Paraguay	Belgium	Iraq	GF	GA	Pt
Mexico	1-1(1-0)	2-1(2-1)	1-0(0-0)	4	2	5
Paraguay		2-2(1-0)	1-0(1-0)	4	3	4
Belgium *			2-1(2-0)	5	5	3
Iraq				1	4	0

Group 3

Team	France	Hungary	Canada	GF	GA	Pt
USSR	1-1(0-0)	6-0(3-0)	2-0(0-0)	9	1	5
France		3-0(1-0)	1-0(0-0)	5	1	5
Hungary			2-0(1-0)	2	9	2
Canada				0	5	0

Group 4

Team	Spain	Northern Ireland	Algeria	GF	GA	Pt
Brazil	1-0(0-0)	3-0(2-0)	1-0(0-0)	5	0	6
Spain		2-1(2-0)	3-0(1-0)	5	2	4
Northern Ireland			1-1(1-0)	2	6	1
Algeria				1	5	1

Group 5

Team	West Germany	Uruguay	Scotland	GF	GA	Pt
Denmark	2-0(1-0)	6-1(2-1)	1-0(0-0)	9	1	6
West Germany		1-1(0-1)	2-1(1-1)	3	4	3
Uruguay *			0-0(0-0)	2	7	2
Scotland				1	3	1

Group 6

Team	England	Poland	Portugal	GF	GA	Pt
Morocco	0-0(0-0)	0-0(0-0)	3-1(2-0)	3	1	4
England		3-0(3-0)	0-1(0-0)	3	1	3
Poland *			1-0(0-0)	1	3	3
Portugal				2	4	2

*These teams went into the next round as the best third place finishers.

Highlights:

Maradona set up all three goals against South Korea in spite of playing with an injury. He volleyed in the equaliser against Italy. Against Bulgaria he set up one of the two goals. The best was yet to come.

England qualified in spite of a goalless draw against Morocco and a shock defeat against Portugal. Interestingly, they would have gone through even if they had drawn against Poland. In this strange group, Morocco emerged as the surprising toppers.

Brazil was still a great team, in spite of the aging stars. And in Careca they had a striker with a voracious appetite for goals.

France and USSR both showed fine form, plenty of scoring power, and played out a memorable 1-1 draw.

And while West Germany started slow, drawing against Uruguay, losing to Denmark and just about getting past Scotland, the Danes showed splendid form in crushing the Uruguayans 6-1 and beating the Germans by a brace of goals.

Second Round

Mexico 2 (1) Bulgaria 0 (0)
Belgium 4 (0,2) USSR 2 (1,2)
Brazil 4 (1) Poland (0)
Argentina 1(1) Uruguay 0 (0)
France 2 (1) Italy 0 (0)
West Germany 1 (0) Morocco (0)
England 3 (1) Paraguay 0 (0)
Spain 5 (1) Denmark 1 (1)

Highlights

The Belgians struck form in the nick of time, coming from behind twice to surge past the impressive Russians in a fascinating encounter.

Brazil's scoreline against Poland suggests that they dominated, but they were helped along by two penalties.

West Germany scraped through past a very impressive Morocco side by virtue of a very late Lothar Matthäus curling freekick.

The Uruguyans, warned by FIFA, could not afford to mark Maradona in the way they wanted to.

The incredible turnaround was Spain's huge win over Denmark. The latter had till then played like genuine champions, but things fell apart for them in this encounter.

Quarter-finals

France 1 (1,1) Brazil 1 (1,1) Tie-Breaker France 4 Brazil 3
West Germany 0 (0,0) Mexico 0 (0,0) Tie Breaker West Germany 4 Mexico 1
Argentina 2 England 1
Belgium 1 (1,1) Spain 1 (0,1) Tie-Breaker Belgium 5 Spain 4

Three out of the four quarter-finals were decided by tie-breakers.

Brazil crashed out after Zico failed to convert a penalty kick in regulation time and Bellone's kick in the tie-breaker went in off the post and the keeper's back.

The campaign of the hosts came to an end after another uninspired West German game had seen the teams locked goalless after two hours of an unclean game.

And then there was the famous showdown between Argentina and England. Maradona leapt for the ball with Peter Shilton and executed the notorious Hand-of-God goal. Ali Ben Nasser, the Tunisian referee, was deceived, and so were most of the spectators in the stadium. Shilton and the English footballers, who saw exactly what took place, were still reeling from the injustice when the Argentinian superstar got hold of the ball in his half, took it all the way, beating four men and wrong-footing Shilton before netting one of the most unbelievable goals of all time. Gary Lineker reduced the margin, but it came a bit too late in the game.

Semi-finals

West Germany 2 (1) France 0 (0)

The cardinal mistake of conceding an early goal against a relentlessly professional outfit did France in. When they got desperate for an equaliser as time started to run out, the Germans scored another through a clinical counter-attack.

Argentina 2 (0) Belgium 0 (0)

It was another Maradona-spectacular. After a goalless first half, the genius scored twice, the second goal almost a replica of his masterpiece against England.

Third-Place Final

France 4 (2,2) Belgium 2 (1, 2)

It was an up and down game, with France coming from behind to seize the advantage, and the Belgians equalising late in the game. But a brace of goals, one of them from penalty, saw France through after regulation time.

Final
Argentina 3 (1) West Germany 2 (0)

Franz Beckenbauer's ploy of using Lothar Matthäus to mark Maradona actually started to pay off. It was a rare Schumacher lapse which saw Judy Brown head in the first goal. And the German goalkeeper uncharacteristically stayed back when Valdano ran in to make it 2-0.

After this, however, Andreas Brehme curled in two corners and using their advantage in the air, they were netted by Rumenigge and Völler. With 14 minutes to go for the final whistle the score was 2-2.

But an astute instant through by Maradona to Burruchaga with five minutes remaining in the game saw Schumacher slow to react and the scoreline showed 3-2. One of the greatest finals ever.

Highlights:

Beckenbauer admitted that he did not have enough players of quality to win the title.

Argentina's Marcelo Trobbiani replaced Burruchaga with one minute remaining in the final. He was on the field for that solitary minute. It is the shortest World Cup career for any footballer.

The France-Belgium match was the first, and till now the only, Third-Place final to go to extra time.

It is Cañedo, not Canedo

According to the rules the game should end now

You should lose all the remaining funds

But I choose to ignore a small blemish. You will move to the next question and the game shall go on. However, 0.5% of your funds are gone forever. You now have **64.5%** of your original amount.

"Oh the Spanish accents!"

"I don't believe it !!"

"Don't blame Mike, Herr F. He was one of your FIFA men. Predecessor. You should have corrected the spelling as he was saying it."

"Let us move on. We could have lost all the remaining. Now we stand at 64.5%."

i. In spite of issuing threats of confiscating the whole amount, he wants to complete the game he has so elaborately composed
ii. Definitely an individual
iii. Fascinated by his own riddles

In the lap of a giant of another day/ David-Goliath is underway

1990, Italy

It was no surprise that Italy became the first European country to host the World Cup twice. What was, however, mildly surprising was that Mexico had already done so.

Gary Lineker managed to play after having recovered from jaundice. Ruud Gullit captained the powerful Dutch side after having been injured for most of the year. However, the gifted Romario broke a leg in March and his World Cup was limited to 66 minutes against Scotland.

The tournament geared up to be a showdown between West Germany and Argentina once again. Glamour was added because of dashing blond strikers in both sides, Claudio Caniggia and Jürgen Klismann. But a suspension to the former, a distinctly low par Maradona, and rather uninspired performance by both the sides, saw one of the most insipid title round in history. The final was decided by a penalty which should never have been given.

First Round

Group 1

Team	Czechoslovakia	Austria	USA	GF	GA	Pt
Italy	2-0(1-0)	1-0(0-0)	1-0(1-0)	4	0	6
Czechoslovakia		1-0 (1-0)	5-1(2-0)	6	3	4
Austria			2-1(0-0)	2	3	2
USA				2	8	0

Group 2

Team	Romania	Argentina	USSR	GF	GA	Pt
Cameroon	2-1(0-0)	1-0(0-0)	0-4(0-2)	3	5	4
Romania		1-1(0-0)	2-0(1-0)	4	3	3
Argentina ?			2-0(1-0)	3	2	3
USSR				4	4	2

Group 3

Team	Costa Rica	Scotland	Sweden	GF	GA	Pt
Brazil	1-0(1-0)	1-0(0-0)	2-1(1-0)	4	1	6
Costa Rica		1-0(0-0)	2-1(0-1)	3	2	4
Scotland			2-1(1-0)	2	3	2
Sweden				3	6	0

Group 4

Team	Yugoslavia	Colombia	UAE	GF	GA	Pt
West Germany	4-1(2-0)	1-1(0-0)	5-1(2-0)	10	3	5
Yugoslavia		1-0(0-0)	4-1(2-1)	6	5	4
Colombia ?			2-0(0-0)	3	2	3
UAE				2	11	0

Group 5

Team	Belgium	Uruguay	South Korea	GF	GA	Pt
Spain	2-1(2-1)	0-0(0-0)	3-1(1-1)	5	2	5
Belgium		3-1(2-0)	2-0(0-0)	6	3	4
Uruguay ?			1-0(0-0)	2	3	3
South Korea				1	6	0

Group 6

Team	Rep. Ireland	Holland	Egypt	GF	GA	Pt
England	1-1(1-0)	0-0(0-0)	1-0(0-0)	2	1	4
Rep. Ireland		1-1(0-1)	0-0(0-0)	2	2	3
Holland ?			1-1(0-0)	2	2	3
Egypt				1	2	2

Rep. Ireland finished second and Holland third after lots were drawn to decide between them. These teams went into the next round as the best third place finishers.

Highlights:

Cameroon stunned Argentina and continued to impress against Romania. 38-year-old Roger Milla came in as late substitution and demonstrated incredible opportunism. His jig near the corner flag is one of the lasting memories of the Cup.

René Higuita, the Colombian goalkeeper, stunned the world by coming out repeatedly and aiding the defence as an additional back. It would come back to bite the side later on, but for now they were an impressive bunch, led by the bushy yellow dreadlocked Carlos Valderamma.

The Colombia-West Germany match was petering into a goalless draw when Littbarski slammed in two minutes from time, only for Rincón to equalise in the injury time.

Brazil looked unimpressive in spite of an all-win sheet.

Maradona's right hand played the divine part this time, saving a goal from USSR in a crucial encounter, once again away from the eyes of the officials.

Neri Pumpido, the Argenitinian goalkeeper, picked up an injury against USSR and gave way to Sergio Goycochea, who would play a stellar role in the Cup.

Peter Shilton emulated Dino Zoff by captaining his side at 40. However, the group of England, Rep. Ireland, Holland and Egypt played some of the drabbest football in the tournament.

Second Round

Cameroon 2 (0,0) Colombia 0 (0,0)
Czechoslovakia 4 (1) Costa Rica 1 (0)
Argentina 1 (0) Brazil 0 (0)
West Germany 2 (0) Holland 1 (0)
Rep Ireland 0(0,0) Romania 0 (0,0) Tie breaker: Rep Ireland 5 Romania 4
Italy 2 (0) Uruguay 0 (0)
Yugoslavia 2 (0,1) Spain 1 (0,1)
England 1 (0,0) Belgium 0 (0,0)

Highlights

It was the wily Roger Milla who sealed it for Cameroon, helped in no small proportions by Higuita's insistence to come out beyond the penalty box.

Maradona, playing with an inflamed toenail, nevertheless started the move that led to Caniggia slamming in a late goal against Brazil. The Brazilians managed to convert just four of the 56 chances they created in the Cup.

Belgium hit the post twice in the first 90 minutes before going down to England in the extra-time.

All through teams found it difficult to score. Some suggested that the size of the goal be increased because the game had evolved.

Quarter-finals

Argentina 0 (0,0) Yugoslavia 0 (0,0) Tie Breaker Argentina 3 Yugoslavia 2
Italy 1 (1) Rep. Ireland 0 (0)
West Germany 1 (1) Czechoslovakia 0 (0)
England 3 (1,2) Cameroon 2 (0,2)

Seven goals were scored in the four quarter finals, five of them in regulation time. Four of them, the West German goal as well two of England's and one of Cameroon's came off penalties. The main attraction of a football match had dried up in this tournament.

Goycochea demonstrated what was in store by winning the shootout for Argentina.

Italy rode the dream run of Salvatore Schillaci.

West Germany were helped by the sending off of Ľubomír Moravčík, after the midfielder had kicked his boot away in disgust.

The England-Cameroon match was fractious and even brilliant at times. Milla came on earlier than usual, at half-time. And the game changed as Cameroon equalised and then took the lead. The penalty which allowed Lineker to make it 2-2 has been debated ever since. The penalty awarded in extra-time was hardly debatable. Lineker sent the goalkeeper the other way and made it 3-2.

Semi-finals

Argentina 1 (0,1) Italy 1 (1,1) Tie-breaker Argentina 4 Italy 3

The Italian goalkeeper Walter Zenga conceded his first goal in 11 matches when Caniggia equalised. But then the sole prolific striker of Argentina handled the ball and was out of the final. Goycochea, the rising star, yet again demonstrated his incredible knack of saving penalties.

West Germany 1 (0,1) England 1 (0,1) Tie-breaker West Germany 4 England 3

It was part lacklustre, but the match went down to become an epic. A battle on knife's edge, with Brehme taking the lead and Lineker equalising, and tensions mounting with Gascoigne receiving the yellow card that would have kept him out of the final if England had made it. Playing the third extra-time in succession, the first ever team to do so in World Cup, England held the Germans to the 1-1 score. But in the tie-breaker, Pearce had his shot stopped and Waddle shot over the bar.

Third-Place Final

Italy 2 (0) England 1 (0)

It was Baggio's cheeky goal, after stealing the ball away from Shilton as he rolled it on the ground, that made the quiet match come to life after 71 minutes. Platt equalised 10 minutes later, and Schillaci became the highest scorer of the tournament with the conversion of the penalty in the 85th minute.

Final

West Germany 1 (0) Argentina 0 (0)

Without Caniggia, and three more suspensions, the Argentinians seemed to bank heavily on the esoteric penalty saving skills of Goycochea. The game was one of the most painful to witness, with one team intent on defence, the other rather uninspired in their attacks.

Finally Völler went down to a tackle, or dived as is the general consensus. The resulting penalty kick was taken by Brehme. Goycochea dived in the right direction, but could not stop it.

Two Argentinian players being sent off also did not help their cause.

It was the first final with the losing side not scoring a goal. Also the first final without a field goal. The first final which saw the spectators glad when it was over.

Highlights:

The 16 red cards was a record in the tournament.

Goals per game was 2.21, the lowest ever witnessed in the World Cup.

David-Goliath ... Argentina reached the final, but they limped quite a bit on their way. Defending champions, they stumbled against Cameroon in the first round.

But, who is the giant of another day?

That is what baffles me.

Well ... that's difficult to say. Giant in any case seems figurative.

Was there a very tall player from a previous World Cup who was watching ...?

Where was it played?

Milan...

Which stadium?

San Siro.

Hang on. It was later renamed to Giuseppe Meazza Stadium ... Meazza, the hero of the 1934 World Cup.

Meazza

In the lap of a giant of another day !

Accents... be careful of the accents.

Right.
You have now moved to the next question

OFFICIAL MEMO
Subject : FIFA 2018
Assignment : SUDDEN DEATH
By : Javier Hernandez

a. Active on niche discussion forums on all these topics …

b. Probable locations
   - East London,
   - Pretoria and
   - Mumbai.

NB :   (Indians have never even played in the World Cup). But they follow sports, have a huge, huge population, and thus a proportional number of crazy football fans.

c. Mobilised agents in all these cities

Replaced fellow apostle after time was up/Yet Him up there won the Cup

_ _ _ _ _   _ _ _ _ _ _   _ _ _

1994, United States of America

Between the World Cups, the Iron Curtain had been raised. USSR had broken down and FIFA had recognised Russia as their successors. And Germany was unified once again.

England and France did not qualify.

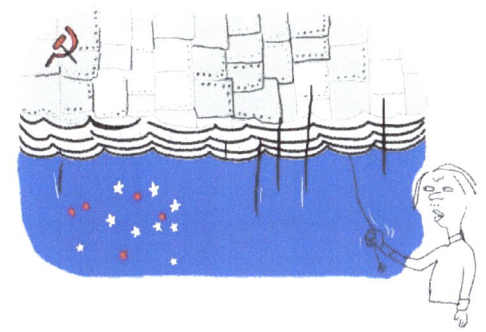

The experiment of hosting the Cup in football-agnostic United States to make it popular in that most powerful of countries was not a real success.
It did draw huge crowds, but it was bracketed by disappointment for the fans at the start and the end.

First, Havelange had the temerity to ban Pelé from the opening ceremony for criticising the head of the Brazilian Football Association, Ricardo Teixeira. It was more than a mere coincidence that Teixeira was the son-in-law of Havelange.

Secondly, the final did not only produce the most defensive and drab football, it was also decided by penalties after the 90 minutes and the extra time had ended goalless.
The tournament also saw tragic and calamitous outcomes. Maradona tested positive during a drug test, just after he was showing signs of regaining something close to his best form. And Andrés Escobar, the Colombian defender, paid the price of his own goal against USA with his life. Someone who had lost a great deal of money because of the defeat shot him dead on his return to his homeland.
For the first time, three points were awarded for a win.

First Round

Group 1

Team	Switzerland	USA	Colombia	GF	GA	Pt
Romania	1-4(1-1)	1-0(0-0)	3-1(2-1)	5	5	6
Switzerland		1-1(1-1)	0-2(0-1)	5	4	4
USA			2-1(1-0)	3	3	4
Colombia				4	5	3

Group 2

Team	Sweden	Russia	Cameroon	GF	GA	Pt
Brazil	1-1(0-1)	2-0(1-0)	3-0(1-0)s	6	1	7
Sweden		3-1(1-1)	2-2(1-1)	6	4	5
Russia			6-1(3-0)	7	6	3
Cameroon				3	11	1

Group 3

Team	Spain	South Korea	Bolivia	GF	GA	Pt
Germany	1-1(0-1)	3-2(3-0)	1-0(0-0)	5	3	7
Spain		2-2(0-0)	3-1(1-0)	6	4	5
South Korea			0-0(0-0)	4	5	2
Bolivia				1	4	1

Group 4

Team	Bulgaria	Argentina	Greece	GF	GA	Pt
Nigeria	3-0(2-0)	1-2(1-2)	2-0(1-0)	6	2	6
Bulgaria		2-0(0-0)	4-0(1-0)	6	3	6
Argentina *			4-0(2-0)	6	3	6
Greece				0	10	0

Group 5

Team	Rep Ireland	Italy	Norway	GF	GA	Pt
Mexico	2-1(1-0)	1-1(0-0)	0-1(0-0)	3	3	4
Rep Ireland		1-0(1-0)	0-0(0-0)	2	2	4
Italy *			1-0(0-0)	2	2	4
Norway				1	1	4

Group 6

Team	Saudi Arabia	Belgium	Morocco	GF	GA	Pt
Holland	2-1(0-1)	0-1(0-0)	2-1(1-0)	4	3	6
Saudi Arabia		1-0(1-0)	2-1(2-1)	4	3	6
Belgium *			1-0(1-0)	2	1	6
Morocco				2	5	0

These teams went into the next round as the best third place finishers.

Highlights:

The Gallon brothers, drug dealing gambling lords, who were responsible for the murder of Escobar were subjected to a ridiculously lenient punishment of 15 months of house arrest. Their bodyguard, Humberto Muñoz, who pulled the trigger, was sentenced to 43 years in prison, later reduced to 26 years, and was ultimately released after serving 11 years.

Mexico, Republic of Ireland, Italy and Norway became the first four teams to end a group in the World Cup with exactly the same points. Rep Ireland ended in the second place because they had beaten Italy, although the goals for and against also matched for the sides.

Argentina, defeated by Colombia 5-0 in the recent past, just about scraped through as did Italy.

However, Maradona, scoring a goal in the World Cup after eight years, tested positive in a drug test and had to return home.

Brazil, was insipid in the mid-field, and rather functional in their defence, was given a spark of life by the combination of Romario and Bebeto in the front line.

Oleg Salenko's five goals against Cameroon remains a record for a single match. In the same game, Roger Milla, 42, became the oldest to score in a World Cup match.

Diego Maradona's 16 matches as captain is a World Cup record

Second Round

Germany 3 (3) Belgium 2 (1)
Spain 3 (1) Switzerland 0 (0)
Sweden 3 (1) Saudi Arabia 1 (0)
Romania 3 (2) Argentina 2 (1)
Holland 2(2) Rep Ireland 0 (0)
Brazil 1 (0) USA 0 (0)
Italy 2 (0,1) Nigeria 1 (1,1)
Bulgaria 1 (1,1) Mexico 1 (1,1) Tie-Breaker Bulgaria 3 Mexico 1

Highlights

Brazil overcame a stiff challenge by USA through a Romario-Bebeto combination in the 74th minute. The Brazilians played with 10 men from the 44th minute after Leonardo had been sent off for elbowing Ramos and cracking his cheekbone.

Italy were given a lease of life against Nigeria by Roberto Baggio who scored the equaliser two minutes from time, and then converted a penalty 12 minutes into the extra-time.

The Bulgaria-Mexico encounter had the potential to be excellent but was ruined by poor decisions by the referee.

An absolutely desperate Preud'homme, the Belgian goalkeeper, running into the German penalty box as a corner was floated in the last minute. But, the Germans held on to the 3-2 advantage.

The best match by far was the Romania-Argentina showdown. The Latin American giants fought hard without Maradona, but had to bow to the brilliance of Ille Dumitrescu and Gheorghe Hagi.

Quarter-finals

Italy 2 (1) Spain 1 (0)
Brazil 3 (0) Holland 2 (0)
Bulgaria 2 (0) Germany 1 (0)
Sweden 2 (0,1) Romania 2(0,1) Tie-Breaker Sweden 5 Romania 4

Brazil took a two goal lead through the Romario-Bebeto genius, following which Bebeto celebrated with baby-rocking. The second goal was disputed, with the Dutch expecting the referee to blow the whistle as Romário was clearly offside. However, they equalised in a quarter of an hour's dominant play which saw some of the best of Denis Bergkamp. The issue was sealed by a 25-yard free kick by the veteran Branco, who had replaced Leonardo for the match.

The most delightful triumph was obtained by Bulgaria, with the Stoichkov free kick and a Lechkov diving header allowing them to come from behind after Germany had taken the lead through a penalty.

Semi-finals

Italy 2 (2) Bulgaria 1 (1)
A Roberto Baggio brace within the space of five minutes, both the goals spectacular, put it beyond the spirited but outclassed Bulgarians.

Brazil 1 (0) Sweden 0 (0)
The Brazilians did win this through a late goal by Romário, but they did find it difficult to break through. It was a precursor of what was to come.

Third-Place Final
Sweden 4 (4) Bulgaria 0 (0)
It was a rather strange result. The Bulgarians had done a lot of good work in the tournament and did not deserve to be the first team to concede four goals in the third-place final.

Final

Brazil 0 (0,0) Italy 0 (0,0) Tie-Breaker Brazil 3 Italy 2
If the 1990 final had been poor, this one tried to match it in every way. For the first time the title-round finished goalless. Both Baggio and Romário missed open nets. In the shootout, Romário's shot went in off the post. Baggio shot over the cross bar.

Highlights:

The midday heat in which some matches were contested sapped the life force out of several teams. This was topped by humidity. Much of this was due to the organisers trying to play ball with television timing.
Bulgaria won a match in the World Cup after 24 years, and kept winning till the semi-final.

Riberio later wrote: "Who won the Cup?" Hinting at the answer "Him up there."

Riberio doesn't fit. Also, what is that about replacing fellow apostle after time was up?

Hmm ... that may be it. Crizam de Oliveira (Zinho) was replaced by Paulo Sérgio Rosa (Viola) in the 105th minute of the match, in the extra time.

After time was up! And it still did not yield a goal. Paulo Sérgio Rosa. Exact fit.

Right. It was the first ever final that ended in a goalless draw ... and proceeded to penalty shootout.

"We can discuss all that later. Let me type that in."

"Oh ... what are you doing?"

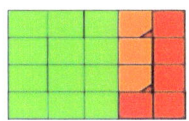

Wrong !

Careless error once again.

It is Sérgio, not Sergio.

Second such error. In all honesty you should lose all your funds now

Yet, I am magnanimous. I will deduct another 0.5%

And you can continue ... but have to solve three clues in 15 minutes the next time.

Look what you've done

OFFICIAL MEMO
Subject : FIFA 2018
Assignment : SUDDEN DEATH
By : Javier Hernandez

a. Suspect definitely wants the game to be completed

b. Perhaps wants to hurry because he knows that we are closing in on him (?)

Mumbai

Pretoria

East London

... two of the three suspects have been rounded up and are being questioned. The third cannot be contacted.

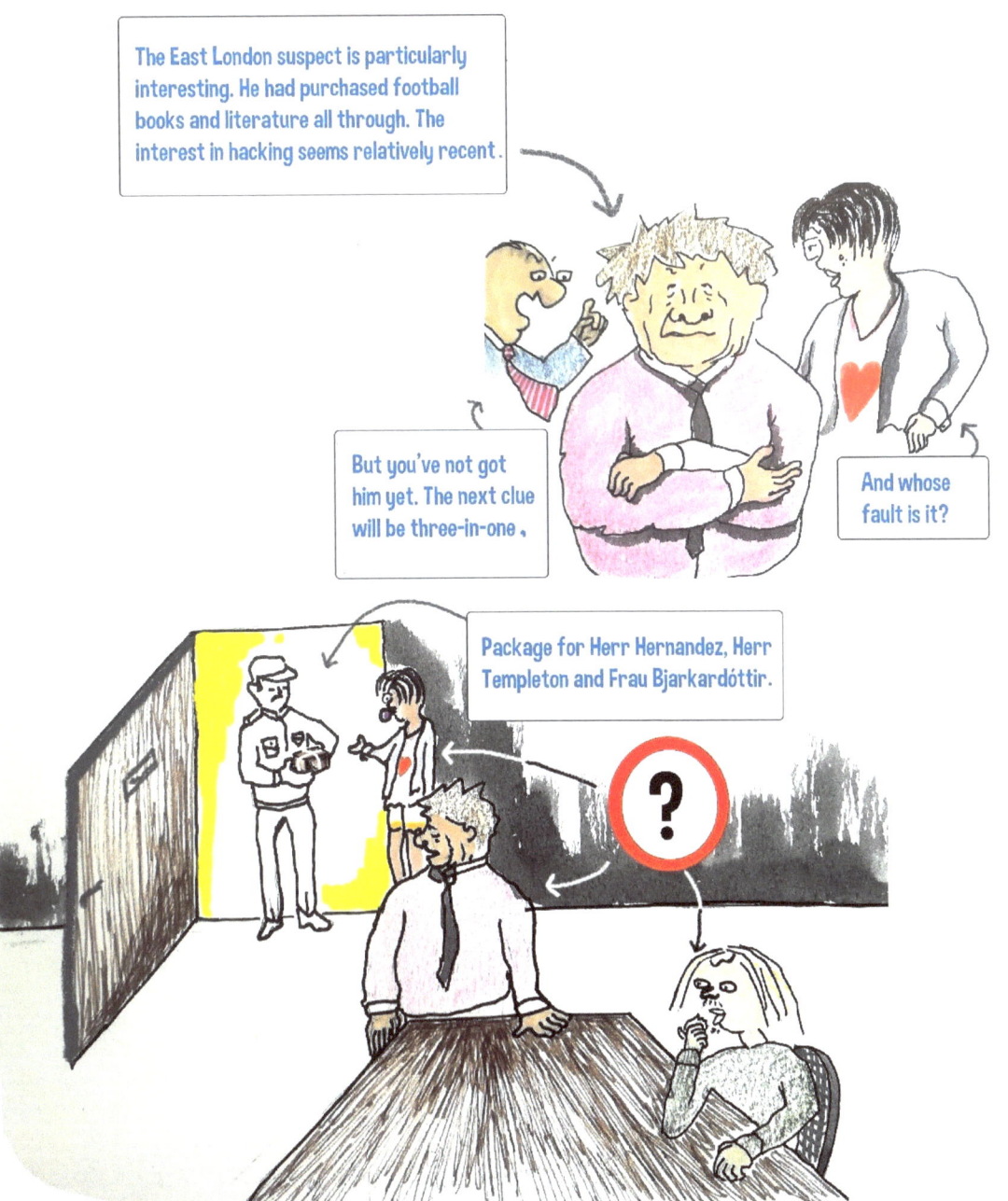

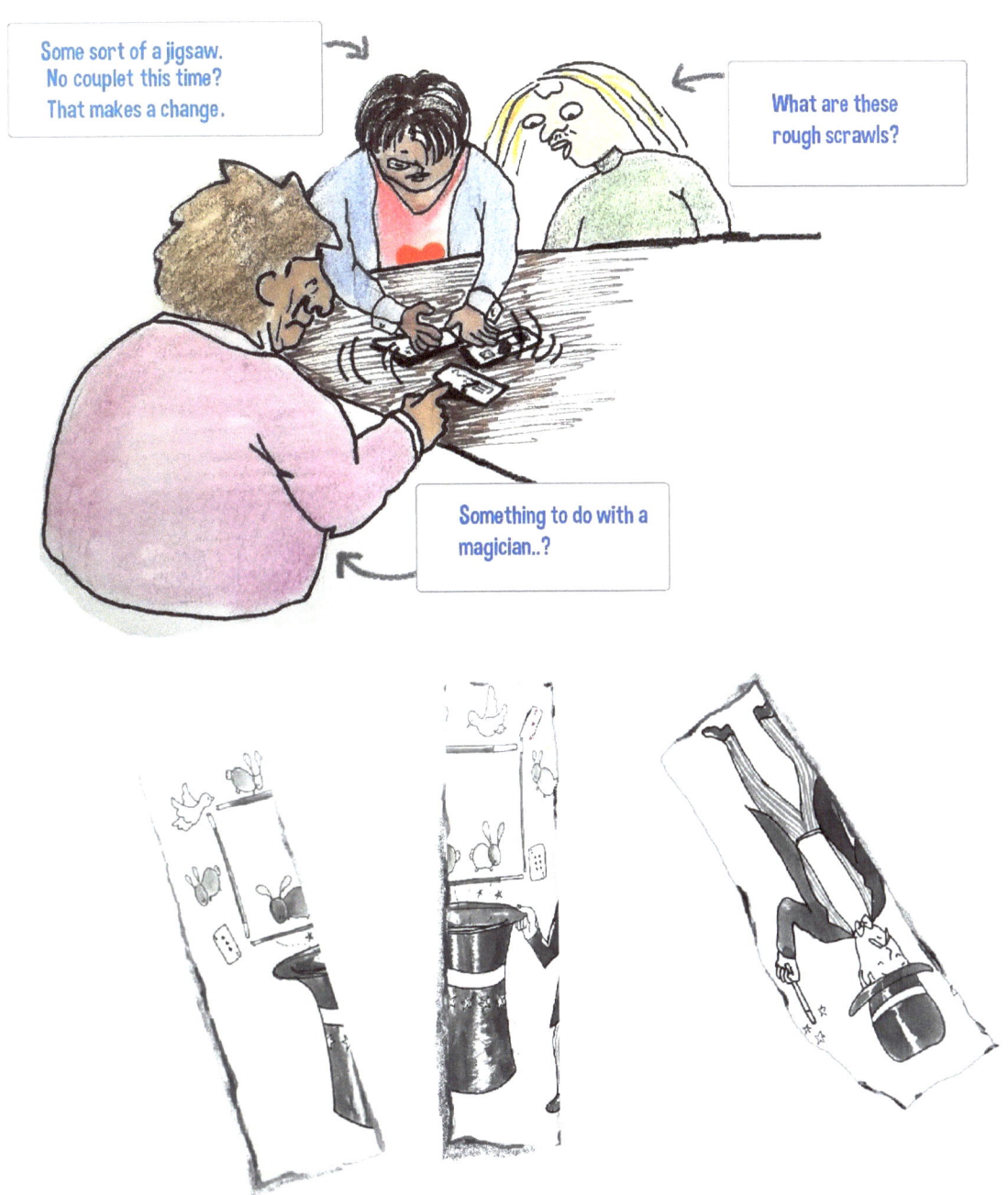

1998, France

At last some good decisions from FIFA.

Tackles from the rear became banned. The injury time board was introduced.

But, now there were 32 teams. It made it mathematically easier, but way more difficult to ensure uniform quality.

2002, Japan and South Korea

For the first time the World Cup reached Asia, although it was split into two hosts. At the same time FIFA reeled with corruption charges against Sepp Blatter. When general secretary Michael Zen-Ruffinen was removed as financial controller after being a whistle-blower, Ken Bates wrote: "The last World Cup under the rotten, corrupt, crooked reign of Blatter... even the monkey from Hartlepool would be an improvement."

Let us look back at 1998, 2002 and 2006

2006, Germany

Germany hosted the Cup after several allegations of bribery and corruption.

A tournament of mixed allure, ending with a riveting climax for the wrong reasons. Zinedine Zidane's head butt was unprecedented, and perhaps forever unique, in the history of the World Cup. But once again the final was decided through penalties, a pain that fans had already gone through in 1994.

Italian Team
2006

1st round

1998, France	2002, Japan and South Korea	2006, Germany
Klinsmann still looked in prime form in the early matches Romário was not in the Cup due to disciplinary reasons, but Ronaldo and Rivaldo started in a fashion that left few in doubt about Brazil being the favourites to win the tournament. However, after FIFA had allowed a wedding between a Norwegian and a Brazilian on the pitch, Norway shocked them 2-1 in the final group match, even though Brazil had taken the lead as late as in the 77th minute. A politically charged Iran-USA match at Lyon was played in the best of spirits with the former winning 2-1. The two countries who would host the next tournament managed just one solitary point between them.	The Uruguay-Senegal match provided a contest as topsy-turvy as can get. Senegal led 3-0 at the breather, Uruguay scored three times in the second half. The Ronaldo, Rivaldo, Ronaldinho brigade started out a trifle slow, but peaked early ... and kept raising the bar. China was the fifth country Bora Milutinovic coached in the World Cup. He had been with Mexico in 1986, Costa Rica in 1990, USA in 1994 and Nigeria in 1998. South Korea surprised all by topping their group. They beat Poland and Portugal while being held, surprisingly, by USA. Using their superior skills in the air, Germany headed in five during their 8-0 rout of Saudi Arabia. Argentina did not go through to the second round, stopped by England and Sweden. Some solace for the English fans still stinging from the 1986 incident	Marco van Basten for the Holland team, Dick Advocaat for South Korea, Guus Hiddink for Australia and Leo Beenhakker for Trinidad and Tobago made four Dutch coaches in the tournament. The major surprise was perhaps Switzerland who upstaged France in Group G. Brazil started with flourish yet again but benefitted from being in a relatively easy group. Portugal looked a strong, dominant side, as did their neighbours Spain. The former had in their ranks a young Christiano Ronaldo. For Argentina, a 19-year-old Lionel Messi made his first foray into the competition

2nd Round

1998 France

Brazil continued their rampage by beating Chile 4-1. In contrast, France just about edged Paraguay through the new concept of Golden Goal. England went out in penalties again, this time to Argentina

2002, Japan and South Korea

87.70% of the German population watched them beat Paraguay with a late goal.

The Rivaldo-Ronaldo show overcame Belgium with a couple of sparks of brilliance in the heat and humidity.

The golden goal came to South Korea's aid after Italy had been up by a goal for most of the match, till the 88th minute.

2006, Germany

Germany blasted past Sweden scoring a brace of goals in the first 12 minutes.

Argentina had to struggle past Mexico in the extra time

The England-Ecuador, Portugal-Netherlands, Italy-Australia matches yielded one goal apiece, Switzerland-Ukraine none.

In contrast the three goals Brazil put past Ghana, and the way France came from a goal down to beat Spain 3-1 were rather refreshing

2002, Japan and South Korea

1998 France	2002, Japan and South Korea	2006, Germany
	Quarter Finals	
France and Italy settled a keenly contested goalless stalemate through penalties. French captain Deschamp's sister Nathalie Tauziat lost the Wimbledon singles final to Jana Novotna the following day. Bergkamp's genius stopped Argentina in a superb showdown. Ronaldo played in spite of tendonitis and fumbled several times, but set up two of the three goals that saw Brazil through against Denmark. And an aging German side was soundly beaten by an enthusiastic Croatia making their debut in the tournament.	Ronaldinho's incredible free-kick sailed over Seaman and, fluke or genius, pipped England 2-1. Turkey overcame Senegal in an unlikely quarter-final match by virtue of a golden goal. Germany, wearing black armbands in memory of former captain Fritz Walter, overcame a dogged USA side.	Miroslav Kolse equalised in the 80th minute and Argentina went out in penalties. It ended in a mass brawl between the players. Another tie-breaker, another English side bowing out. This time to the Portugese. And after yet another goalless draw. An aging Roberto Carlos was blamed by many when Thierry Henri scored in the 57th minute. Cafu's numerous runs into the French half did not quite manage the needed equaliser.
	Semi Finals	
Brazil had to resort to penalties to overcome one of the best Dutch sides in history. Ronald de Boer was thoroughly rebuked by his twin Frank when his kick was stopped. Croatia's dream run ended when Thuram equalised within a minute of Sûker's goal, and then nudged in the winner	Brazil overcame a determined Turkish side, pipping them by the Ronaldo goal. Towards the end they brought in Denilson, and one was treated to the sight of four defenders trying desperately to take the ball away from the dribbling phenomenon. Germany also managed just a goal against South Korea, and rode quite a bit on the brilliance of Oliver Kahn.	After being locked goalless for 119 minutes, during the last couple of minutes in the extra time Italy scored twice to oust Germany. Zidane converted the penalty that took France to the final past Portugal as veteran Thuram had another superb match.

Final		
A strange affliction to Ronaldo, who insisted on sleepwalking through the match even after his epileptic fit, was appended by a brilliant Zidane. The result was a 3-0 rout, helped along by one of the worst ever performances by a defence line in a final.	Ronaldo redeemed himself with sustained genius, while after a superb tournament Kahn finally proved human. The 2-0 win meant the fifth Cup for Brazil, and the fifth straight time that the losers had failed to score in a World Cup final since it happened for the first time in 1990.	After early excitement, the longer the final went on, the more likely it seemed to be decided through penalties. In the last stages, a Zidane header, on the ball and not Materazzi, was tipped one-handed by a desperately lunging Buffon.

**1998
France**

"The Dutchman, Guus Hiddink"

"Trust the Dutch to do something odd like this ... There another perfect fit."

... And abracadabra !
Well done ... You've got all three.
You have now recovered 89% of the money.

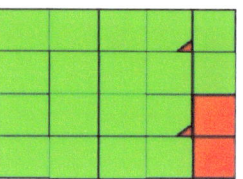

"That is a 1-2-1 formation !"

Can the team crack this cryptic puzzle? Can they recover the rest of the money? Or will the World Cup be in jeopardy?

Who is this curious adversary they are up against? Will he play fair?
To find out more you must read the last volume of SUDDEN DEATH

1998, France

First Round

Group 1

Team	Norway	Morocco	Scotland	GF	GA	Pt
Brazil	1-2(0-0)	3-0 (2-0)	2-1 (1-1)	6	3	6
Norway		2-2(1-1)	1-1(0-0)	5	4	5
Morocco			3-0(1-0)	5	5	4
Scotland				2	6	1

Group 2

Team	Chile	Austria	Cameroon	GF	GA	Pt
Italy	2-2(1-1)	2-1(0-0)	3-0(1-0)	7	3	7
Chile		1-1(0-0)	1-1(1-0)	4	4	3
Austria			1-1(0-0)	3	4	2
Cameroon				2	5	2

Group 3

Team	Denmark	South Africa	Saudi Arabia	GF	GA	Pt
France	2-1(1-1)	3-0(1-0)	4-0(1-0)	9	1	9
Denmark		1-1(1-0)	1-0(0-0)	3	3	4
South Africa			2-2(1-1)	3	6	2
Saudi Arabia				2	7	1

Group 4

Team	Paraguay	Spain	Bulgaria	GF	GA	Pt
Nigeria	1-3(1-1)	3-2(1-1)	1-0(1-0)	5	5	6
Paraguay		0-0(0-0)	0-0(0-0)	3	1	5
Spain			6-1(2-0)	8	4	4
Bulgaria				1	7	1

Group 5

Team	Mexico	Belgium	South Korea	GF	GA	Pt
Holland	2-2(2-0)	0-0(0-0)	5-0(2-0)	7	2	5
Mexico		2-2(1-0)	3-1(0-1)	7	5	5
Belgium			1-1(1-0)	3	3	3
South Korea				2	9	1

Group 6

Team	Yugoslavia	Iran	USA	GF	GA	Pt
Germany	2-2(0-1)	2-0(0-0)	2-0(1-0)	6	2	7
Yugoslavia		1-0(0-0)	1-0(1-0)	4	2	7
Iran			2-1(1-0)	2	4	3
USA				1	5	0

Group 7

Team	England	Colombia	Tunisia	GF	GA	Pt
Romania	2-1(0-0)	1-0(1-0)	1-1(0-1)	4	2	7
England		2-0(2-0)	2-0(1-0)	5	2	6
Colombia			1-0(0-0)	1	3	3
Tunisia				1	4	1

Group 8

Team	Croatia	Jamaica	Japan	GF	GA	Pt
Argentina	1-0(1-0)	5-0(1-0)	1-0(1-0)	7	0	9
Croatia		3-1(1-1)	1-0(0-0)	4	2	6
Jamaica			2-1(1-0)	3	9	3
Japan				1	4	0

Second Round

Italy 1 (1) Norway 0(0)
Brazil 4(3) Chile 1(0)
France 1 (0,0) Uruguay 0(0,0)
Denmark 4 (2) Nigeria 1 (0)
Germany 2 (0) Mexico 1(0)
Holland 2 (1) Yugoslavia 1 (0)
Croatia 1(1) Romania 0(0)
Argentina 2(2,2) England 2 (2,2) tie-breaker Argentina 4 England 2

Quarter-finals

France 0 Italy 0 tie-breaker France 4 Italy 3
Brazil 3 (2) Denmark 2 (1)
Holland 2 (1) Argentina 1(1)
Croatia 3 (1) Germany 0 (0)

Semi-finals

Brazil 1 (0,1) Holland 1 (0,1) tie-breaker Brazil 4 Holland 2
France 2 (0) Croatia 1 (0)
Third-Place Final
Croatia 2 (2) Holland 1 (1)

Final

France 3 (2) Brazil 0 (0)

First Round

Group 1

Team	Senegal	Uruguay	France	GF	GA	Pt
Denmark	1-1(1-0)	2-1(1-0)	2-0(1-0)	5	2	7
Senegal		3-3(3-0)	1-0 (1-0)	5	4	5
Uruguay			0-0(0-0)	4	5	2
France				0	3	1

Group 2

Team	Paraguay	South Africa	Slovenia	GF	GA	Pt
Spain	3-1(0-1)	3-2(2-1)	3-1(1-0)	9	4	9
Paraguay		2-2(1-0)	3-1(0-1)	6	6	4
South Africa			1-0(1-0)	5	5	4
Slovenia				2	7	0

Group 3

Team	Turkey	Costa Rica	China	GF	GA	Pt
Brazil	2-1(0-1)	5-2(3-1)	4-0(3-0)	11	3	9
Turkey		1-1(0-0)s	3-0(2-0)	5	3	4
Costa Rica			2-0(0-0)	5	6	4
China				0	9	0

Group 4

Team	USA	Portugal	Poland	GF	GA	Pt
South Korea	1-1(0-1)	1-0(0-0)	2-0(1-0)	4	1	7
USA		3-2(3-1)	1-3(0-2)	5	6	4
Portugal			4-0(1-0)	6	4	3
Poland				3	7	3

Group 5

Team	Rep Ireland	Cameroon	Saudi Arabia	GF	GA	Pt
Germany	1-1(1-0)	2-0(0-0)	8-0(4-0)	11	1	7
Rep Ireland		1-1(0-1)	3-0(1-0)	5	2	5
Cameroon			1-0(0-0)	2	3	4
Saudi Arabia				0	12	0

Group 6

Team	England	Argentina	Nigeria	GF	GA	Pt
Sweden	1-1(0-1)	1-1(0-0)	2-1(1-1)	4	3	5
England		1-0(1-0)	0-0 (0-0)	2	1	5
Argentina			1-0(0-0)	2	2	4
Nigeria				1	3	1

Group 7

Team	Italy	Croatia	Ecuador	GF	GA	Pt
Mexico	1-1(1-0)	1-0(0-0)	2-1(1-1)	4	2	7
Italy		2-1(0-0)	2-0(2-0)	4	3	4
Croatia			0-1(0-0)	2	3	3
Equador				2	4	3

Group 8

Team	Belgium	Russia	Tunisia	GF	GA	Pt
Japan	2-2(0-0)	1-0(0-0)	2-0(0-0)	5	2	7
Belgium		3-2(1-0)	1-1(1-1)	6	5	5
Russia			2-0(0-0)	4	4	3
Tunisia				1	5	1

Second Round

Germany 1 (0) Paraguay 0 (0)
England 3 (3) Denmark 0 (0)
Senegal 2 (1,1) Sweden 1 (1,1)
Spain 1 (1,1) Rep Ireland 1 (0,1) tie-breaker Spain 3 Rep. Ireland 2
USA2 (1) Mexico 0 (0)
Brazil 2 (0) Belgium 0 (0)
Turkey 1 (1) Japan 0 (0)
South Korea 2 (0,1) Italy 1 (1,1)

Quarter-finals

Brazil 2 (1) England 1 (1)
Germany 1 (1) USA 0 (0)
South Korea 0 (0,0) Spain 0 (0,0) tie-breaker South Korea 5 Spain 3
Turkey 1 (0,0) Senegal 0 (0,0)

Semi-finals

Germany 1 (0) South Korea 0 (0)
Brazil 1 (0) Turkey 0 (0)

Third-Place Final

Turkey 3 (3) South Korea 2 (1)

Final

Brazil 2 (0) Germany 0 (0)

First Round

Group 1

Team	Ecuador	Poland	Costa Rica	GF	GA	Pt
Germany	3-0(2-0)	1-0(0-0)	4-2(2-1)	8	2	9
Ecuador		2-0(1-0)	3-0(1-0)	5	3	6
Poland			2-1(1-1)	2	4	3
Costa Rica				3	9	0

Group 2

Team	Sweden	Paraguay	Trinidad n Tobago	GF	GA	Pt
England	2-2(1-0)	1-0(1-0)	2-0(0-0)	5	2	7
Sweden		1-0(0-0)	0-0(0-0)	3	2	5
Paraguay			2-0(1-0)	2	2	3
Trinidad n Tobago				0	4	1

Group 3

Team	Holland	Ivory Coast	Serbia & Montenegro	GF	GA	Pt
Argentina	0-0 (0-0)	2-1(1-0)	6-0(3-0)	8	1	7
Holland		2-1(2-1)	1-0(1-0)	3	1	7
Ivory Coast			3-2(1-2)	5	6	3
Serbia & Montenegro				2	10	0

Group 4

Team	Mexico	Angola	Iran	GF	GA	Pt
Portugal	2-1(2-1)	1-0(1-0)	2-0(0-0)	5	1	9
Mexico		0-0(0-0)	3-1(1-1)	4	3	4
Angola			1-1(0-0)	1	2	2
Iran				2	6	1

Group 5

Team	Ghana	Czech Republic	USA	GF	GA	Pt
Italy	2-0(1-0)	2-0(1-0)	1-1(1-1)	5	1	7
Ghana		2-0(1-0)	2-1(2-1)	4	3	6
Czech Republic			3-0(2-0)	3	4	3
USA				2	6	1

Group 7

Team	France	South Korea	Togo	GF	GA	Pt
Switzerland	0-0(0-0)	2-0(1-0)	2-0(1-0)	4	0	7
France		1-1(1-0)	2-0 (0-0)	3	1	5
South Korea			2-1(0-1)	3	4	4
Togo				1	6	0

Group 8

Team	Ukraine	Tunisia	Saudi Arabia	GF	GA	Pt
Spain	4-0 (2-0)	3-1(0-1)	1-0 (1-0)	8	1	9
Ukraine		1-0(0-0)	4-0(2-0)	5	4	6
Tunisia			2-2(1-0)	3	6	1
Saudi Arabia				2	7	1

Second Round

Germany 2 (2) Sweden 0 (0)

Argentina 2 (1,1)Mexico 1 (1,1)

England 1 (0) Ecuador 0 (0)

Portugal 1 (1) Holland 0 (0)

Italy 1 (0) Australia 0 (0)

Ukraine 0 (0,0) Switzerland 0 (0,0) tie-breaker Ukraine 3 Switzerland 0

Brazil 3 (2) Ghana 0 (0)

France 3 (1) Spain 1 (1)

Quarter-finals

Germany 1 (0,1) Argentina 1 (0,1) tie-breaker Germany 4 Argentina 2

Italy 3 (1) Ukraine 0 (0)

Portugal 0 (0,0) England 0 (0,0) tie-breaker Portugal 3 England 1

France 1 (0) Brazil 0 (0)

Semi-finals

Italy 2 (0,0) Germany 0 (0,0)

France 1 (1) Portugal 0 (0)

Third-Place Final

Germany 3 (0) Portugal 1 (0)

Final

Italy 1 (1,1) France 1 (1,1) tie-breaker Italy 5 France 3

A Product of the Blinders Team

www.ingramcontent.com/pod-product-compliance
Lightning Source LLC
LaVergne TN
LVHW071032070426
835507LV00003B/123